One Tiny Baby

WRITTEN BY MARK A. TAYLOR
ILLUSTRATED BY SCOTT BURROUGHS

Published by Standard Publishing, Cincinnati, Ohio
www.standardpub.com

ISBN 978-0-7847-2295-4

15 14 13 12 11 10   2 3 4 5 6 7 8 9 10

Standard®
PUBLISHING

Cincinnati, Ohio

One tiny baby—
see him on the hay?

Two smiling people—
hear Mary say,

"We are very happy
with this little one.
His name is Jesus,
God's only Son."

Three fuzzy donkeys
may have rested there.

Or four nosy puppies
may have sniffed the air.

Five sleepy cows
may have wondered why
their quiet stable
heard a baby's cry.

Six woolly lambs
may have watched to see
seven strong men
falling on their knees.

Eight cooing doves,
perched overhead,
also see the baby
in his manger bed.

Nine busy spiders,
spinning webs with care,
pay no attention
to Jesus sleeping there.

But ten noisy roosters,
when the night is done,
seem to crow together,
"God has sent his Son!"